Steve

THE
MIND
OF A
TENNIS
PLAYER

A Guide to the
Mental Side of the Game

ISBN: 1522874569
ISBN 13: 9781522874560

I would like to dedicate this book to my wife, Mary. Her love and support transcends all boundaries.

Table of Contents

Acknowledgements

I would like to thank all of my family members for allowing me to take the time to write this book. My inspiration came from my wife, who has encouraged me over the years to write about my many experiences pertaining to the mental side of the game of tennis. I have had an incredible journey, and I am thankful that I found the time to put my thoughts into words.

Over the past four decades, I have actively competed in a number of leagues and tournaments. I have experienced many emotions and been confronted with a number of mental struggles. I wrote this book to share these experiences with you and provide you with some valuable information on how to conquer the tennis demons we all encounter. If you experience concentration issues, irrational fears, on-court anxiety, or tension, this book can be of great assistance. If worrying has kidnapped you from the joy you have experienced in playing this great game, this books for you.

As a teaching professional, I have also been immersed in the mental battles of many of my students. I have learned a variety of strategies for combatting the anxiety and stress of competition. In this book I provide you with a number of personal examples where I failed the mental test but learned from my loss. Over time these experiences have allowed me to become a mentally tougher competitor.

I also discuss the importance of selecting the right teaching professional for you. This is so important if you want your game to progress consistently.

I look forward to sharing with you some keys to developing a strong mental game. I sincerely hope this book enables you to make your tennis experiences more enjoyable.

One

I grew up in a small city sixty miles south of Rochester, New York. In Hornell, it always seemed like we had an extremely long winter accompanied by a very short spring, summer, and fall. As a young boy, I had my heart set on being a professional basketball player. I used to sleep with my basketball and dream about playing against some of my favorite professionals. Hornell's Maple City Park had a basketball court, tennis courts, baseball and soccer fields, pool, and playground. I spent countless hours on the basketball court, anticipating a great future in the game.

Then one day something interesting happened. I was shooting baskets at the park when an older gentleman came up and asked me if I would like to hit some tennis balls with him. He said he had an extra racket, so I agreed, and we took the short walk to the tennis courts. His name was Jim Oyer, and I had no idea what a positive impact he was going to have on my life.

Soon we began to hit, and it became obvious that Jim was a seasoned tennis player. Fortunately I had some athletic ability, so I was able to hit some balls back to him. Then he asked me if I would like to play a couple of sets. I told him that I would, but that he might have to help me with the some of the rules and scoring procedures. He agreed and the match began. It didn't take long for the first set to come to an uneventful end. In the second set, I began to find a little bit of rhythm (even though I had no clue about correct stroke technique), so we had some longer rallies. Nonetheless, I lost the match 6–0, 6–0. I thanked him for letting me use his racket and told him I would be interested in playing again if he could put up with me. He laughed and said, "How about tomorrow?" Of course I said yes. Little did I know that I was about to embark on an incredible journey.

Jim and I started playing on a regular basis. I continued to play basketball, but I soon realized that my heart had been stolen by a game called tennis. As I became a better player, Jim began to take me to some of the tournaments he played. He became a good friend and left me with many memorable experiences.

Now I am fifty-seven years old and have experienced many peaks and valleys over the last four decades. I would probably never have written this book if I hadn't recently had foot surgery. For the last month, I have lain in bed with my foot up on two pillows. Maybe this surgery was a blessing in disguise. It has given me the opportunity to share with you many of the game-shaping experiences I have encountered over the years. At one point in my life, my mental struggles forced me to lay my racket down. The self-imposed pressures became overwhelming. Playing tennis was no longer fun anymore. In this book, I will share with you the tools I used to recapture the pleasure I once experienced playing this great game.

Two

What Tennis Is Really All About

So what is tennis really about? First and foremost, it is about having fun. You try to become the best player you can. You take lessons, engage in match play, and participate in hitting drills in order to raise your level of play. Unfortunately, too often we lose sight of what it is all about. We begin to worry about what others think of our game. We become afraid of losing our spot on our United States Tennis Association team. We shy away from tournament play because of that disabling fear, the fear of losing. In our minds, losing a tennis match becomes an unbearable proposition. Subsequently our tennis game suffers. We've lost our way.

Tennis is a challenging game. First let's talk about the scoring system. You can easily be ahead 6–1, 3–0 in a tennis match and still end up losing. Looking at this in mathematical terms, it means you're up nine games to one before you meet your demise. In some other sports, a 9–1 lead would almost be insurmountable. However, it doesn't work that way in tennis. You are always under pressure. You always have to work hard to win that next point. I remember one of my first tournament matches many years ago, playing an area high school tennis coach. The first set went by quickly, and in the second set I wasn't showing any signs of making it a competitive match. Being down 0–6, 0–5, I didn't see any light at the end of the tunnel. But I told myself to just keep playing hard. Then suddenly I won a game. Delighted and surprised, I persevered, fighting for every point. Now I was only down 4–5 and just played on freely, realizing that the match should have been over twenty minutes ago. I won the next game and recognized that my opponent was beginning to self-destruct. I went on to win that set and subsequently the match. From that day forward, I realized that I needed to play every point just one point at a time. A tennis match is truly not over until it is over, fight for every point to the end.

Driving home, I began to think about what had just occurred. I remembered the immense joy I felt when I won the very last point of the match. Then I recalled the look on my opponent's face when we shook hands at the net. How must he have felt when he lost that last point? Did he have an intense feeling of failure? Or did he just chalk it up to a bad day? The wheels in my brain were turning.

Let's talk about this match, which took place approximately forty years ago. First we need to get back to the tennis scoring system. I was behind 0–6, 0–5, but I ended up the winner. Even after losing eleven straight games, I still prevailed. In the game of tennis, you always have to be mentally and physically prepared to battle and win that next point. You are never able to relax and enjoy the scenery. Each and every point is important. Second, this match opened my eyes to the importance of mental strength, focus, and perseverance. I learned to keep fighting regardless of the score. The match is never over until that last point is won or lost. On this day I won the mental battle; later in this book, we will revisit some matches where I was less fortunate.

So what is tennis really about? It is about looking forward to hitting with a friend on a particular day. It is about working on a weakness with your teaching professional. It is about looking forward to a league or tournament match. It is about enjoying the on-court battle. It is about staying aggressive and focused when closing out a match. But when all is said and done, it is really about your enjoyment in being part of this great game. Boris Becker once said, "I love the winning, I can take the losing, but most importantly I love to play."

Whether you go out and hit with a friend or participate in leagues or tournaments, it is all about enjoying the experience. If you compete, the joy comes in battling for every point and finally letting the chips fall where they may. Think about it: you have two or four players, a racket with strings, a can of balls, and a rectangular court that you try to keep the ball in. That is all it is. Tennis was developed as, and still is, a game. There is nothing wrong with wanting to win, but learn to accept defeat as graciously as you relish victory. For a number of years I was unable to do that. Winning was great, but losing was devastating. Now I congratulate my opponent when I'm defeated and look forward to my next opportunity to compete.

In the remainder of this book, I will discuss the many challenges I experienced as a competitor. Through all the ups and downs, I have always remained passionate about the game.

Three

CHANGE YOUR PERSPECTIVE ON LOSING

Unfortunately, losing a match can have a crippling effect on a player. It can make the competitive experience less enjoyable if you allow it to. It is imperative to overcome the fear of losing if you want to fulfill your potential as a tennis player.

Years ago, when I lost a league or tournament match, I steamed over that loss for days. It was a major occurrence in my life. It was almost like I had to beat myself up for a few days before I could go back to having fun on the court again.

There are many ways the fear of losing creeps into your tennis life. You become concerned about:

1) Losing a spot on your USTA, high school, or college team

2) Lowering your current National Tennis Rating Program level
3) Disappointing parents and friends
4) Losing to a lower-ranked (or -rated) player
5) What other people will think of you if you lose
6) Dealing with the blow to your confidence
7) Losing to a friend
8) Losing to a player you dislike
9) Losing to a player significantly older than you
10) Losing to a player significantly younger than you

The harsh reality is that if you are dwelling on any one of the above fears prior to a league or tournament match, you cannot play your best tennis. Let's look at a personal example. Years ago I was at a tournament, preparing to play my upcoming match. Meandering around the tennis facility, I encountered a number of players I knew. A few asked me whom I was playing, and when I told them, they all assured me that I would win the match easily. This made me a little tense, because I knew my opponent had some decent wins recently.

Well, my opponent and I warmed up, and shortly thereafter the match began. After the first few games, I realized that the match was going to be very challenging. My mind began to race: *What if I lose to this guy? Everyone thinks I should win easily. This is going to be a tough loss to take.* I began to tighten up. My eleven-ounce racket felt like it weighed ten pounds. I became very tentative with my shots. I fell prey to that disabling fear—the fear of losing.

It used to be that when I lost a tournament match, I thought about all the time and effort I had put into practice matches and sessions. I began to add up all the money I was spending going from tournament to tournament. I thought about all the energy I was putting into my fitness program. I often ended up asking myself, "Is this all really worth it?" Losing a tennis match conjured up so many negative thoughts. Unfortunately, I had lost my way.

Dwelling on a loss simply lengthens the time it will take you to accomplish your tennis goals. It does no good to sit at home stewing over a match outcome. I know players who will take a number of days or even weeks off after a tough loss. You may want to take a day or two off, but then it is back to your tennis goals. If you are physically fatigued, of course, that is a whole other issue. Listen to your body and take off the time you need. However, if you are just brooding about a bad or tough loss, it is time to quit indulging in self-pity and get back on your horse.

Always remember, losing a tennis match is not that important. Some players have a tendency to attach their self-worth with winning and losing. This should never happen. Losing a tennis match has no relationship whatsoever to whom you are as a person. Sometimes we all need to take a step back and reflect on why we play. Again, tennis is just an incredibly fun game.

It's helpful to understand that losing a tennis match can become a positive experience. This was an important lesson that I learned a number of years ago. When you win a match, you are excited. Your tendency is to relish the victory, and how you played during the match becomes irrelevant. You may keep the victory in your heart and mind for a day or two; you are proud of your win, as you should be. On the other hand, shortly after you lose, you begin to dissect the match. You think about what you could have done differently. Did you not play aggressively enough when the match was tight? Did you not come to the net enough? What other strategic changes should you have made? Now you have a true learning experience. Losing helps us become better tennis players. The bottom line is that you learn more from your losses than your victories. Venus Williams once said, "Winning is motivating, but I learn more from my losses." Losing is part of the game, so learn something from it and move on. Most importantly, stay focused and keep working hard. Your goal is simply to get better.

To end this chapter on losing, I would like to reflect on a quote by the great Rafael Nadal, who said, "Losing is not my enemy. Fear of losing is my enemy." Don't ever let the fear of losing take ownership of your tennis life.

Four

No Worries

Let's distinguish between negative thoughts and worrying. Negative thoughts are fleeting and temporary. You play a point and say to yourself, *My backhand is terrible today,* and then the next point begins. But when you worry, you dwell on something that can only have a detrimental impact on your game. Worry becomes the center of your thoughts. It stays in your mind for an extended period of time. Worrying is most common prior to and after a league or tournament match. You may worry for a couple days about whom you'll play in an upcoming tournament match. Or if you lose, you may worry about the loss for a few days. Worrying can have a major impact on how you play in future matches, and it may ultimately result in your abandoning competitive play entirely.

To reach your true potential as a tennis player, you have to set your tennis worries to the side. What do I mean by tennis worries? Players spend way too much time focusing on the what-ifs: *What if I lose this match? What if my ranking drops? What if I let my partner down?* The list goes on and on. Worrying prior to, during, and after a match serves no constructive purpose. It zaps you of your energy and your desire to compete. The bottom line is that you cannot reach your true potential unless you get control of this tennis demon.

Let's go back to an earlier chapter to illustrate this. In one of my first tournament matches, I was trailing 0–6, 0–5, but somehow I won. Let's dissect that match a little bit.

There I was, a sixteen-year-old, skinny-legged boy playing for the love of the game. I was running side to side, just trying to return as many balls as possible, smiling whether I won or lost the point. I had nothing to prove to anyone. Whether I won or lost the match, I still would have remembered the pleasure I received in playing the great game of tennis. Win or lose, it was a wonderful experience.

Let me tell you what happened next. I practiced hard and became a much better tennis player. I took the game very seriously, and I began to win more and more matches. All of a sudden I was winning tournaments, and I became the best tennis player in our county. The local newspaper ran a page-long story about all my accomplishments.

Sounds like a storybook ending, right? Well, it was far from it.

I became consumed with worry. It came to the point where I worried about my reputation at every tournament I played. I had thoughts like, *If I lose this match, my ranking will drop. All this work I have done will have been a waste of time. What are people going to think if I lose to this guy?* The list went on and on. I would begin to dwell on these things, and soon I wasn't having fun playing anymore. I began to lose more and more matches. Winning was everything and losing was gut-wrenching. It was time to quit playing tennis.

After a few weeks of my self-imposed hiatus, I began to realize how much I missed hitting the tennis ball. I knew that I truly loved the game, but I also realized that I couldn't go back to the way it was. I decided to take some time and put my thoughts on paper. After twenty minutes or so, I came up with three specific strategies that I knew I had to adhere to at all times if I was going to get back out on the court:

1) First and foremost, my focus will be to enjoy playing the game of tennis. No longer will I worry about my rating, ranking, or reputation. I will play for me.

2) When I play a league or tournament match, I will no longer worry about my opponent's rating,

ranking, or reputation. I will be competing against a faceless player.

3) After losing a league or tournament match, I will devote thirty minutes to dissecting and analyzing the loss. I will write down a few things that I can take to the practice court, and I will complete my checklist (which we will talk about in a later chapter). Once the thirty minutes has expired, the defeat becomes ancient history.

After implementing these strategies for a few tournament matches, I realized that I had discovered the right path. I began to enjoy competing and could smile on the court again. I still wanted to win each match I played, but losing became much more tolerable.

Today I have come full circle. I am back to being that sixteen-year-old boy who loved the game of tennis. I can't wait to play now, because all of the worries and what-ifs are buried forever.

You need to take your tennis worries, lock them in a box, and throw away the key. Try the above strategies if you struggle with this tennis demon. You may also want to come up with some strategies that are more specific to your own worries.

Five

Identify and Remove the Tension Indicators

In order to play your very best tennis, you need to relax. It is very difficult to reach your potential if you are playing with an elevated level of tension. It is unfortunate that people play for years and never conquer this tennis demon. They are simply unable to overcome it because they have no idea on what strategies to implement. Consequently, it continues to deprive them of playing their best tennis.

There has been much written on the mental side of the game of tennis. There are articles and books on how to dismiss or redirect negative thoughts, maintain a positive attitude, improve confidence, and many other valuable topics. All of this information can help us become mentally tougher on the court. It is good stuff, and this book concentrates on much of this information.

Regrettably, there are not enough articles or books that identify the *physical behaviors* one exhibits when competing under an elevated level of nervous tension. I call these on-court behaviors "tension indicators." Here are the top ten indicators you may have experienced at one time or another:

1) Shallow breathing
2) Not moving your feet
3) Muscling the tennis ball
4) Rushing between points
5) Becoming tentative on some of your shots
6) Exhibiting negative body language
7) Exclusively playing defensive tennis
8) Beginning to have an erratic ball toss on your serve
9) Verbally reprimanding or belittling yourself
10) Leaning or stepping back to hit your ground strokes/volleys

If you have experienced an elevated level of tension on the court, it is very important that you and/or your coach identify the specific tension indicators that need attention. These tension indicators may only become evident at certain times in the match. You may only experience these problems in the first few games of the first set, or when closing out a match.

Over the last thirty years I have seen each of these ten tension indicators in action. Now I want to give you some important information on how to identify and remove them. Let's get started.

Tension Indicator #1
You engage in shallow breathing

Have you ever been in the heat of tennis battle and your breathing has become rapid and shallow? Your breathing patterns alone can dictate your level of play. Ideally, you should inhale through your nose and exhale through your mouth. Exhale when you make contact with the ball. Between points, take a few deep breaths and make a quick strategic change if needed. Make sure these deep breaths come from the lower abdominal region. I recommend you take three deep breaths and then a fourth just prior to serving. You should also focus on your breathing during the changeover. I believe that deep breathing is one of the most effective methods you can use to relax your body.

Years ago I was confronted with a serious breathing problem. I was playing a tournament match and began to gasp for air at end of almost every point. I knew that my physical fitness level was not an issue, but I was still unable to identify the source of the problem. I finally realized that I was holding my breath during each point. My breathing had become so labored that playing to my potential was not even remotely possible. Always make sure you exhale at ball contact.

Tension Indicator #2
You stop moving your feet

It is a lot easier for a coach to identify this than it is for the player himself. I have found that when a player is competing, his footwork becomes one of the last things he thinks about. When a match gets tight, your feet suddenly become glued to the asphalt. When you hit the ball, you end up just standing there hoping that your shot isn't returned back in play.

Let's look at a few things you can do to make sure that your footwork is in proper order. First, make sure you consistently come back to an explosive "ready position." You should have a low center of gravity, positioned on the balls of your feet and standing with your feet not less than shoulder-width apart. Second, make sure you split step (a little hop on two feet and return to the ready position) when your opponent is bringing his racket forward to strike the ball. Third, begin to move to the ball as soon as you can determine the direction the ball is taking. Don't wait to see if the ball is going wide, long, or into the net before you start to move. You want to begin to move in the direction of the ball as soon as you see it leaving your opponent's racket.

Focus on these three keys when you are drilling or playing practice matches. They have to become embedded in your mind. When you get into a tight situation in a match, your nerves can take hold of you and your feet stop moving. When that time arrives, you may want to remind yourself of these three keys.

Tension Indicator #3
You are muscling the tennis ball

It is very important that your hitting arm remains loose and relaxed. This begins with how your hand is gripping the racket. You want to hold the handle only as tightly as you must to keep the racket in your hand. You don't want to hold the racket with what many call a death grip. When a match gets close, we become more susceptible to holding the racket too tightly. Your goal is to maintain a relaxed arm so that your stroke can remain smooth and effective. Your best opportunity to accomplish this is to keep your grip loose and your hitting arm relaxed. When you grip the racket too tightly, your stroke becomes restricted and you end up muscling the tennis ball.

Once a point is over, transfer the racket to your opposite hand until the next point is ready to begin. You may want to shake your hitting arm a few times before you return the racket to your dominant hand.

Tension Indicator #4
You are rushing between points

For some players, the tighter the match becomes, the faster they get ready to play the next point. They become very tense and try to lower their level of tension by removing themselves from the stressful situation as quickly as possible. Don't get me wrong, they still want to win as badly as their opponent does. It is just that they want to rid themselves of their elevated level of tension. The correction is to slow down and concentrate on your breathing and between-point/changeover rituals. You cannot play your best tennis if you are rushing between points and on the changeovers.

Tension Indicator #5
You are becoming tentative on some of
your shots

The score is 4–4 in the third set. You have been playing some great tennis, and you see the end in sight. You really want to win the match. You hit out on your forehand, but on your backhand you are becoming more defensive. Up to this point in the match, you had been effectively hitting out on your backhand side. You end up losing the match 7–5 in the third set. You leave the court and begin to wonder why you didn't continue to hit out on your backhand when the third set got tight. You also remember a couple times at the net when you didn't put the ball away when you had the opportunity. Sound familiar? When you get to this point in the match, you start to realize that the end is near, and this can create a higher level of nervous tension. Remember your breathing, but also remember the type of play that got you to this point in the match. Trust your strokes when the match gets tight. Hit out on your shots, and stay focused until the last point has been played. You want to give yourself the best opportunity to win. If you hit out on your shots and do lose, it becomes much easier to accept!

Tension Indicator #6
You are exhibiting negative body language

Your body language on the court has to be positive. Once you engage in negative body language, your level of play will usually take a noticeable dip. Always display the appearance that you are the only player on the court who is going to win the match. When a match gets tight, maintain a positive external appearance regardless of your emotions and thoughts. You know that the match isn't over until the last point is won. We will discuss this indicator more in the next chapter.

Tension Indicator #7
You are exclusively playing defensive tennis

As a coach, I think this tension indicator has always irritated me the most. I have had students who hit aggressive ground strokes with me during their lesson with an above-average level of consistency. Then, when I attend one of their league or tournament matches, it is like I am seeing a completely different player. They start to push the ball on almost every shot. This is so frustrating to me because I know they can play so much better tennis. When we meet again, I am completely up-front and honest with them. I let them know that they were playing too defensively during the match. I remind them that their goal is to get better and that I can't help them unless they are willing to believe in their strokes and hit out on the ball. I ask them to think back to our last lesson, when we were consistently hitting aggressive forehands and backhands with each other. I also remind them that this didn't change when we played a few points at the end of the lesson.

Players who experience this problem are too outcome oriented. They experience an elevated level of tension and reduce their game to a level of play well beneath them. How they hit the ball is irrelevant. They want to win so badly that improving as a player is not a part of their big picture.

If at any point in the match you begin to play in a solely defensive fashion, remind yourself that your goal is to become the very best tennis player you can be. This will not happen unless you adhere to the right game plan. Believe in your strokes and hit out on the ball.

Tension Indicator #8
You begin to have an erratic toss on your serve

Having a consistent change in your ball toss often indicates an elevated level of tension. The tossing arm becomes very tight and fails to extend all the way up on the delivery. Usually this results in a low ball toss. Subsequently you will have more missed first serves and double faults. I am a big believer in taking a deep breath directly prior to serving. This will help to keep your tossing arm loose.

You may need to shake this arm a few times to release some tension. Make sure your tossing arm extends all the way up on the delivery. Also, the tossing hand should not squeeze the ball too tightly. This will result in your ball toss becoming erratic.

When you become tense, you may begin to grip the racket too tightly on the serve. Your serving arm has to be loose and relaxed like your ground strokes. When you are squeezing the grip too tightly, you muscle your serve and its effectiveness lessens.

Tension Indicator #9
You verbally reprimand or belittle yourself

Tennis can be frustrating if you allow it to be, and that frustration, accompanied by the pressure of the moment, can compel you to berate yourself. But if reprimanding or belittling yourself allowed you to play a higher level of tennis, it wouldn't be a tension indicator. The problem is that your game suffers when you criticize yourself verbally. It serves no positive purpose. You should never verbalize any of your negative thoughts. I believe it is best to remain quiet and calm throughout the match. I used to express both positive and negative emotions, but I soon realized I was wasting much-needed energy. I believe an occasional fist pump is fine, but to play your best tennis, you need to be calm and relaxed.

Tension indicator # 10
You are leaning or stepping back on your ground strokes/volleys

You want to strike the ball in front of your body consistently. When you are experiencing nervous tension, you let the ball come to you. Often this forces you to lean or step back when executing the stroke. Now you are back to playing defensive tennis. Remember, the sooner you get to the ball, the easier it becomes to hit an effective stroke. Make sure you attack the ball with your feet and play to win.

When you are feeling the pressure, make sure you stay aggressive. You need to see the ball come off your opponent's racket and to react immediately. Once you get in position to hit the ball, make sure you have an offensive mind-set. If your goal is to stay aggressive, there is a good chance that leaning or stepping back on your strokes will become a nonissue.

Sometimes players don't notice that their tension level is elevated. They are engrossed in the match, possibly playing too fast between points, and are not thinking clearly and addressing the tension issue. This is one way the list of tension indicators is so valuable. A coach or friend can help identify them, and you can plan a course of action for removal.

When you are experiencing an elevated level of tension, your game suffers. If you feel that nerves are getting the best of you during match play, have a coach or friend watch a couple of your league or tournament matches to determine if you are exhibiting any of these tension indicators. Once these indicators have been identified, follow the advice here to remove them permanently. Simply recognizing an indicator may be enough to eliminate it, or you may have a strategy of your own.

Six

When Faced with Adversity

Sometimes unplanned events occur in a match, resulting in a player experiencing unforeseen stress. Your forehand begins to consistently sail long, your backhand completely leaves you, you begin to double-fault, or your opponent is playing unbelievable tennis. Maybe you can't even find a rhythm on any of your strokes. You begin to doubt your abilities, and your head begins to hang.

It is very easy to stay positive when everything is going well in a match. You can smile and take pride in all of the good shots you are hitting. The tennis ball looks larger than ever, and it is easy to place the ball where you want it. You win the match and leave the court grinning from ear to ear. Now let's talk about the match where things aren't going so well. Let's assume you cannot find any rhythm on your ground strokes. You begin to make a series of unforced errors, lose the first set 2–6, and are soon trailing in the second set 0–2. Now comes the true test of your character. Are you going to throw in the towel and chalk it up to a bad day, or are you going to pull it together and keep fighting?

First, begin to shuffle your feet prior to serving and returning serve. You have to clear your mind of all the negativity and focus only on the ball. Make sure you are taking some deep breaths and not rushing between points. When things aren't going well, it is very important that you find a way to dig deep and draw on everything you have to bring out the best in your game. Forget about the score, past mistakes, and missed opportunities and begin playing one point at a time. Really believe that your rhythm will come back and the momentum will soon change.

Great players find a way to maintain a positive attitude when faced with adversity. You will notice that after Rafael Nadal loses the first set, he rises from his chair after the changeover and sprints to the opposite baseline to start the next set. He knows that the match is far from over. He knows that until the last point has been played, he always has a chance to win. Many times over the years, I have seen a player who is down a set and a couple of breaks of serve in the second set, come back to win the match. You always have a chance.

Let's talk about controlling negative thoughts. We are more prone to experiencing them when we are faced with adversity, and there are a variety of ways to deal with them on the court. What is most important is that you find an effective way to dismiss these thoughts as they pop into your head. You don't want to expend any energy on anything that is counterproductive to reaching your ultimate goal, which is to give yourself the opportunity to play your very best tennis.

I tried a number of methods, and the one that finally worked for me was quite simple. After a point had been played and the negative thoughts reared their ugly heads, I went back to the baseline and began to shuffle my feet for a few seconds before I played the next point. This physical action worked wonders for me. All of a sudden my negative thoughts began to disappear. My mind became clear and my attitude became more positive.

You also can simply dismiss the thought or replace it with a positive one. For example, if you find yourself thinking, *My forehand is horrible today*, you can tell yourself instead, *Keep hitting your forehand. It will come around.* What is most important is to come up with a workable solution that will enable you to remove the negative thoughts you encounter on the court. This is often accomplished through trial and error. It might take some time, but it is a necessary investment.

Next I want to discuss the body language you exhibit on the court. Let's expand on what we discussed in the last chapter. Your body language should remain positive from the first to the last point. Are you a player who hangs your head after you lose an important point? Do your shoulders drop and your steps become heavy? In between points, I recommend that you keep *your steps brisk and light and your head and shoulders up*, especially when you are faced with adversity. It is very important to perform these behaviors during practice matches as well. The way you carry yourself has a direct impact on how you play. You cannot control whether you win or lose, but you can control your attitude and body language on the court. When you complete a match, think back and determine if you maintained a good attitude and exhibited positive body language, especially when faced with adversity. If not, make it a point to work on this before your next match.

There are no strategies that will guarantee a win in every match, of course. You can stay positive when faced with adversity, and you can adopt and implement all of the mental strategies discussed here, and still lose to a lower-ranked player. Roger Federer, arguably the best male tennis player to play the game, once stated, "Sometimes you have to accept that a guy played better on the day than you." It happens to everyone; you are not alone. That being said, I do believe that the mental strategies and other information shared in this and other books will help you win more often. However, you still are going to lose matches that maybe you shouldn't have lost. The goal of this book is to allow you to play your best tennis on a more consistent basis. Accomplishing this will result in your winning more matches and reducing the number of bad losses. On occasion, even the best players in the world lose to much lower-ranked players. It happens; you are in good company.

On a similar note, I have always contended that a mentally tough competitor can admit when his opponent is simply a better tennis player than he is. This is a sign of a competitor who gets it. If another player is noticeably more skilled than you, resulting in a quick and convincing loss, why not admit to others and yourself that he is a better player than you are right now? Why is this considered a sign of weakness? A player who can make this admission understands the nature of competition and possesses a stronger chance of reaching his true potential as a competitor.

You may never have employed any strategies to effectively deal with the challenges presented in this chapter. You are welcome to start with my advice. If you take your tennis seriously, as I do, you'll want to do whatever it takes to consistently play your very best tennis. Maintain a positive attitude from the first to the last point. Remember, the tennis scoring system allows you to always have an opportunity to come back in a match. It is never over until the last point has been won or lost.

Seven

Implementing Five Simple Concentration Keys

Every point in a tennis match is very important. As I said before, the scoring system doesn't allow you to become complacent. You can be ahead 6–0, 3–0 and still end up losing the match. You can never let your guard down. You have to stay focused from the first to the last point.

Below are five simple keys that I highly recommend to help you avoid problems with focus and concentration.

1) Attend to your court and your court alone
2) Develop and adhere to your rituals
3) Silence your mind—only focus on the ball during the point
4) Stay in the moment—forget past mistakes
5) Don't mentally take off points

1) Attend to your court and your court alone

Your concentration and focus should be entirely on the court where you are playing. Looking to another court to see how a friend is playing, or frequently glancing at the crowd to see who is present, results in poor concentration. Between points you can focus on your breathing and look at your racket strings so that your eyes and mind don't wander. You need to give your full attention to the task at hand: playing your very best tennis. When your attention moves away from your court, your ability to remain absorbed in your match is greatly compromised.

2) Develop and adhere to your rituals

A player should have specific rituals he follows between points. For example, I transfer my racket to my other hand immediately after the point has ended. I make sure I take four deep breaths, with the last breath taken immediately prior to serving. I decide on the ball placement, bounce the ball three times, and execute my serve. It is very common to rush between points when you are anxious. Performing rituals between points enables you to slow down and stay in a more focused and relaxed state. Always remember to take a few deep breaths between points, and make sure you have a set routine on changeovers. It's also very important to stay hydrated. I make sure I drink enough water, focus on my breathing, and consider whether I need a strategy change on the changeovers. Depending on where I am in the match, I may also have some fruit or a protein bar to boost my energy.

3) Silence your mind—only focus on the ball during the point

You cannot play your best tennis when your mind is racing. During the point, only concentrate on the ball and where you want to place it. Your opponent's reputation, rating, and ranking are irrelevant. Focus on the ball as it leaves the faceless player's racket, studying that ball closely as you get in position to execute your next stroke. Remember, always trust your strokes and hit out on the ball.

4) Stay in the moment—forget past mistakes

The past is in the past; don't waste time or energy on previous mistakes. To maintain a high level of concentration, you have to stay in the present. You cannot let a bad mistake adversely affect your play for the next two or three games. You can't let it affect you for the next two or three points! It's over, and wasting time and energy thinking about it serves no positive purpose. Staying in the present gives you the best opportunity to play to your potential. A bad call, careless mistakes, and missed opportunities need to be erased from your mind immediately. What is important is the next point!

5) Don't mentally take off points

This goes hand in hand with staying in the moment. There are times in a match when you may let your guard down and mentally withdraw. Let me give you a couple of examples. When you are serving and the score is 40–0, you may have the tendency to lose focus and waste the next point. Your level of intensity drops and your mind may wander. You know you have two more opportunities to hold serve, but if that game score becomes deuce, the wasted point becomes critical. This also occurs when you are winning the set handily. All of a sudden every point is not that important to you. Again your mind wanders and your intensity level drops. You lose that sense of urgency, and your play reflects it. Subsequently your opponent wins a couple of games and the momentum begins to shift. Those squandered points could result in a set lost.

The Mind of a Tennis Player

The next time you play, make a concerted effort to focus on each and every point. Understand that every point is important. A few points could decide the fate of your tennis match. Determine if you have a difficulty with any of the keys discussed above. If you do, make the effort to come up with a game plan to get you back on the right path.

Eight

CONFIDENCE: GET OFF THE ROLLER COASTER RIDE

I was in my early twenties, and I was playing some of my best tennis. I had won a number of tournaments that summer, and my confidence level was at an all-time high. When fall came around, I decided to play in a very challenging tournament that was held in another state. I was ready to play. When I arrived at the tournament site, a friend told me that an Association of Tennis Professionals Tour player was home for the weekend and participating in the tournament. Apparently he had been training with a prominent professional player who was ranked among the top ten in the world. After our discussion, I walked over to take a look at the draw, and I realized that if I won my first match, I would end up competing against him. The following day, I won, and I was really looking forward to what I considered to be the big showdown. As the match time approached, I was a little nervous but very excited. We soon began to warm up, and I was impressed with how cleanly my opponent hit the ball. The match began, and after a few points I realized that this guy could really play. I told myself to stay calm and keep fighting. Well, the match didn't last too long. I lost 6–1, 6–2, and my initial shock was soon followed by unbelievable disappointment. My confidence wasn't just shaken, it was shattered. Within a three-hour period, my confidence level went from an all-time high to an all-time low. It was a crippling experience.

At that point in my life, I had a big problem. I was simply unable to cope effectively with losing a tennis match. After a loss, I would come up with reasons why I shouldn't attend my future practice sessions. I would think about going back to basketball and putting my tennis game on the back burner for a while. It was simple: if I won a tennis match, I became more confident, and if I lost, I became devastated. I was on a never-ending roller coaster ride, and it became a painful road to travel. Looking back on this, I can't believe how immature my thought process was. And think of what I could have learned by dissecting this particular match! After the loss, I should have determined what my opponent had done so much better than I and then taken that information to the practice court. That would have resulted in a true learning experience. The bottom line is that he was simply a better tennis player than I was. Today I could accept that; back then I could not.

In order to build my confidence, I knew I needed to direct my thought processes away from winning and losing and redirect my energy into a workable solution. I finally decided to just focus on my play and let the chips fall where they may. This was difficult for a while, but I knew I needed to be persistent. I realized that I could not control the outcome of a match, but I could control a number of significant factors that affected my play, like my breathing, commitment to hitting out on the ball, intensity of my practice sessions, and ability to stay consistently focused. After a league or tournament match, I asked myself a short list of yes-or-no questions:

1) Did I implement my rituals?
2) Did I give 100 percent effort from the first to the last point?
3) Did I consistently stay focused during the match?
4) Did I believe in my strokes and hit out on the ball?
5) Did I stay positive even when faced with adversity?
6) Did I make a strategic change when I needed to?
7) Were my practice sessions prior to this match intense enough?

After I had answered these questions, I wrote a few comments on what strokes or strategies I needed to work on.

My next step was to make a shift in my thought process. I tried very hard to make the above questions the foundation of my confidence until I participated in my next league or tournament match. Don't get me wrong, I still experienced disappointment when I lost, but winning was no longer the centerpiece of my tennis life. Answering these questions made losing much more bearable. I knew I had to diminish the importance of winning and elevate the importance of focusing on controllable behaviors. The above list was very instrumental in helping me to accomplish this. If I answered no to any of the questions, I deserved to take a blow to my confidence, because these are all attitudes and behaviors I can control. If I could answer yes to each question, I really never had a bad or tough loss. My opponent just played better than I did on that particular day. Once I was able to accept this, I began to look forward to competing again.

You may want to compose a checklist or questionnaire of your own. I highly recommend it. Try to base your level of confidence on how you answer questions like the ones I have provided above. Again, if your current level of confidence is based solely on winning and losing, your ability to enjoy and succeed in this game will become greatly compromised.

As I stated earlier, you will have some good wins and some of what you might label as bad losses. There is a strong chance you will lose to players who are rated or ranked lower than you. There is a strong chance you will lose to a player who is less skilled than you. This is simply a part of the game. I recently had a player inform me that a mutual friend was no longer playing competitively because he lost to a player he felt he was superior to. This isn't that uncommon. I have taught a number of players over the years who had a very difficult time dealing with a tough loss. They could have put their rackets in storage and moved away from tennis entirely. But they learned to overcome the blow to their confidence.

Always remember, it is extremely important that you learn to play for yourself. Never be concerned about what other people think of your game, rating, or ranking. Don't compare yourself to other players. Don't worry about a friend receiving a higher rating or ranking than you. *You need to keep your focus on reaching your potential as a tennis player. This is all that matters in your tennis life.* Remove all thoughts and behaviors that are counterproductive to reaching this goal.

Before I end this chapter, I want to turn our attention to the player who is experiencing confidence issues due to recent match results. As a coach, when I notice a student is experiencing self-doubt because of a series of losses, I have a specific method I use when we discuss it. Let's call this player Jane. Our conversation would go something like this:

Me: "I want you to do me a favor, Jane. Think back to your most recent good win and tell me when it occurred."

Jane: "Well, I beat Rhonda six weeks ago in our second league match."

Me: "Yes, you were hitting the ball so well six weeks ago, and we both know you haven't forgotten how to hit that same ball in that short period of time. You are just thinking about it too much. No problem, Jane. I have had this same issue, and so have many other players. We will work through this together. I have some good ideas for us. Let's get started."

What I want to accomplish here is for Jane to realize that her issue isn't in her physical game, but rather in her mental one. If I can do this, it is so much easier to get her to believe in her strokes again soon. She will stop playing defensive tennis because her confidence is low. She will realize that her forehand and backhand are not the problems, but rather that a change in her thinking needs to take place. Yes, she may have a minor stroke technique issue we can attend to if needed, but the real problem is her diminished level of confidence due to recent match results. Our conversation allows me to forego spending a lot of time practicing serves, forehands, backhands, and the other strokes and instead to focus on Jane's level of confidence. I need her to buy into this so valuable time isn't wasted. We need to get Jane back on the right track as soon as possible. Soon we can implement a post-match checklist focusing on controllable behaviors relevant to her needs, accompanied by other confidence-building exercises.

Finally, let's get off the roller coaster by removing winning and losing as your confidence determinants. Your performance on the court depends on this. Whether you win a tournament or league match or simply defeat a friend, take pride in your accomplishments. You deserve to pat yourself on the back once in a while. When you start feeling tense, take a step back and remind yourself that tennis is just a game and you are playing to enjoy the experience. None of us are playing in the US Open this year. When you play again, keep your thoughts positive and enjoy the battle. Remember, all you can do is stay focused and keep fighting until the last point has been played.

Nine

Be Open to Productive Change

Sometimes you have to move out of your comfort zone to play better tennis. You may need to focus on improving a specific stroke or your footwork, or possibly on implementing a new strategy. This can be difficult and stressful at times. You want immediate improvement, hoping that your game will rise to the next level by the weekend. Here is where you have to change your thought process. Improving in this game takes time and effort. You have to make a commitment to the area you want to improve and set aside the time to practice. Unfortunately, here is what often happens. Let's say your forehand is your weaker stroke, the one that has a tendency to let you down in a match, especially when the set is close. You take a couple of lessons with your teaching professional and are happy with the changes you made. You have a couple of practice sessions, accompanied by some match play implementing the change. Everything is looking good. Now you are ready for your tournament match. You begin play, and for the first few games your forehand is better. Then suddenly at 4–4 you begin to feel the pressure and decide to bring out the old forehand for the remainder of the match. You really want to win and are concerned that the new forehand may break down in the next game or two. The end result is that you've failed to make the commitment necessary to improve your forehand.

I think we have all fallen into this trap at one time or another. To really make a change permanent, it has to carry over from the practice court to the tournament court. You have to be able to put it on the line when participating in an important match. If you are unwilling to do this, moving up a level in the game will become a very difficult proposition.

An intense desire to win can become your biggest obstacle to improvement. Because you want to win, you fall back into the old habits that have hindered your progress. You have to be willing to make a commitment to change, realizing that what is important is where your tennis game is in six months, not tomorrow. If you can improve on one or two aspects of your game every few months, you will be playing tennis at a higher level before you know it. You have to see the big picture. In order to improve, you have to make a commitment to change.

Over the years I have taught a number of students who have been resistant to productive change. If you believe in what your teaching professional is telling you, and his or her advice is working during the lessons, commit to change—and be prepared to handle the short-term aggravation it may create.

There are four sequential steps you need to follow if you really are committed to making a change in a specific stroke.

1) Have your teaching professional work with you on developing the necessary technique change. Practice it in your lessons.
2) Devote time to applying this change in your own practice sessions.
3) Apply the change in practice matches.
4) Apply the change in league or tournament matches.

Once you develop a clear understanding of the change you want to make, integrate it into your practice sessions. When you begin to become comfortable with the change in these sessions, it is time to implement it in practice matches. The final step is to apply it in your league and tournament play.

It is very difficult to improve if you only hit tennis balls once or twice a week. If you are currently playing just once a week, your game will most likely be on a downward slope.

If you play twice a week, you are on more of a maintenance schedule: your game will not improve, but it also won't get worse. If you really want to experience improvement, you need to play at least three times a week.

When you eliminate a weakness in your game, you can add one more feather to your cap. The more feathers you accumulate, the faster you move up to the next level. Weaknesses don't have to be physical; you may have some mental challenges that need to be addressed. You may have a fear of losing or a concentration issue. Work with your teaching professional and come up with an effective game plan. Make the commitment to get better through productive change.

Ten

Don't Stagnate: It Is Time for Goal Setting

Oftentimes players stagnate at a specific level. They only engage in the style of play that allows them to be successful in the league they play in. For example, let's say you are a competing at the 3.0 level in your league. You are winning matches by just focusing on keeping the ball in play. You are very consistent, but your play is defensive. A day comes when you want to compete against a 3.5 level player to see where you stand. Well, upon hitting with this player, you realize that playing a defensive game will not be enough to succeed at this level. He has the ability to hit his shots more aggressively and place the ball where he wants more consistently. You soon realize that you cannot compete at the 3.5 level, so you go back to your 3.0 league and rely on your existing game to win some more matches.

Let's take a look at another example. Let's assume that a player is at a 4.0 level. She hits the ball aggressively but struggles with her second serve, which is flat and fairly slow. She has been able to be effective even with this second serve, however, because she has penetrating ground strokes and volleys. One day she decides to take the opportunity to compete against a 4.5 rated player. They begin to play, and she quickly realizes that when she misses her first serve, her opponent hits the ball aggressively to either corner of the court on her second serve. She is consistently on the defensive and starts to lose her service games. She decides that the 4.0 level is where she should remain.

First let's take a look at the 3.0 level player. If his primary goal was to improve, he would have been hitting out on his shots during his matches. This would have given him the best opportunity to become a better tennis player. However, his primary goal was to win every match he played. Winning took precedence over improving. Again, I am not saying that you shouldn't care if you win or lose. What I am saying is to let winning take second place to improving. This will give you the best opportunity to reach your full potential as a player.

Now let us take a look at our 4.0 player. If over the past year or two she made the effort to develop an effective second serve with spin, she would very likely be at the 4.5

level today. But she knew she could get away with her ineffective second serve at her current level, so improvement wasn't necessary.

Let's discuss something that is extremely important. When drilling, or when playing practice, league, or tournament matches, you have to hit each stroke the way it should be hit. If you get a floater at the net, you need to hit an offensive high-drive volley. If you consistently just tap the ball over the net on this shot, your high-drive volley will not improve. If you get a short-to-midrange overhead, you need to hit it aggressively. If you just consistently guide it back to your opponent, your overhead will not improve. If you have a very flat, slow second serve, you need to develop an effective second serve with spin. If you stay devoted to your existing second serve, you will not improve.

These are just a few examples. You do not want to stagnate at your current level. Get out of your comfort zone and make a commitment to improving. You and your teaching professional should work together to develop some goals that will give you the best opportunity to move forward in your game. Roger Federer once said, "There is no way around the hard work. Embrace it. You have to put in the hours because there is always something you can improve. You have to put in a lot of sacrifice and effort for sometimes little reward, but you have to know that, if you put in the right effort, the reward will come."

Now let's turn our attention to goal setting. I am a big believer in setting performance-based goals (goals you have control over). Examples of these types of goals are:

1) I will concentrate on taking a few deep breaths between points.
2) I will stay positive when my game is struggling.
3) I will hit my approach shots more aggressively.
4) I will develop an effective second serve with spin.

Again, these are all types of goals that you have control of and are unlike outcome -based goals. These are simply goals you do not have any control over. They are completely outcome oriented. Take a look of some examples below:

1) I will win two out of the next four tournaments.
2) I will win eight out of my ten league matches this year.
3) I will beat Sarah in the club championship.
4) I will win a national championship

By setting performance-based goals, you are able take control of your game. You and your teaching professional can set some short- and long-term goals that meet your needs. On the other hand, outcome-based goals can create unnecessary stress, which may result in your becoming disenchanted with the game. I would never recommend setting a goal that you have no control over. Focus on implementing performance-based goals instead.

Finally, make "improving" the focal point of your tennis game. Winning is nice, but reaching your true potential as a player is what it is really all about. Again, I compete and I want to win every match I play. However, my primary focus is to become the best player I can be. Really make the effort to set up some performance-based goals with your teaching professional.

Eleven

IT'S MATCH DAY: PREPARE TO EXCEL

I magine you are on your way to your tennis match and are running late. You stop at a convenience store to get an energy drink and quickly get back on the road. You are fortunate that the traffic is light, and you realize that your arrival time will not be an issue after all. You end up making it to the tournament site twenty minutes before your scheduled playing time. You are relieved. But as your match time approaches, you are worried about the nervous tension you are experiencing. You tell yourself that you have to win this match, and this self-imposed pressure forces you to begin to worry about your play. *Am I going to have a bad day? Will my opponent be a lot better than me?* You walk around the courts aimlessly, worried about the many obstacles you may have to confront. It is now five minutes before the match begins, and your tension level continues to rise. You tell yourself to calm down, but you are unable to remove your nervous tension. As you begin your warm-up, your racket seems heavy and your feet feel like they're in cement.

Has this happened to you? If so, don't be discouraged. The above scenario is not that uncommon. Let us take a step back and we can walk through an effective preparation for match day. This routine will provide you with the opportunity to play your best tennis.

After a good night's sleep and a healthy breakfast, check your tennis bag (which you've packed the night before) to make sure you have everything you need for your match. Make sure you have your fluid of choice, and allow yourself ample time to arrive at the tournament site. You need to be there at least forty-five minutes prior to your scheduled match time. When you arrive, check out the courts to determine their condition, looking for cracks in the asphalt, water on the courts, etc. Make sure all your restroom needs are met. You are going to be a little nervous, but this is completely normal. Feel free to talk to your friends when they arrive. This helps to take your mind off the tension you may be experiencing. Then begin to focus on your breathing, and find a quiet spot to engage in some positive self-talk. I tell myself, *Today is going to be a big day, and I am really looking forward to competing. Win or lose, I am going to play some great tennis.* This helps me to relax and become more comfortable with competing.

Thirty minutes prior to the match, start your pre-match warm-up. You should go for a short jog to warm up your muscles, and after you've worked up a light sweat, you should do some simple stretching exercises. This is followed by a few minutes of jumping rope so your feet can begin moving at a quicker pace.

Fifteen minutes prior to the match, get on the court and hit a few balls with a friend. Make sure you concentrate on your breathing (exhaling at contact), and focus on the ball as it approaches you. I try to read the Wilson or Penn logo on the ball. Concentrate on reading the ball off your opponent's racket, and make sure your feet are active. You should hit some groundstrokes, volleys, overheads, and serves. After these strokes have been completed, you can end this warm-up session.

Finally, a minute or two prior to the match, take a few deep breaths and again engage in some positive self-talk. *Today I feel great, and I know I am going to play well. Win or lose, I am ready to compete.* You are now ready to play some great tennis!

In my self-talk sessions, I always mention three words: *win or lose.* These three words relax me. They take all the emphasis off winning and place it back on competing. This game is all about playing to the best of your ability. You can only give your best effort, focusing on one point at a time. Take any emphasis on winning out of your self-talk sessions. This will allow you to become more relaxed and increase your pleasure in competing.

Again, give yourself the opportunity to play your very best tennis. Don't arrive ten minutes prior to match time and hope that all will go well. Always make sure you enter the match fully prepared to compete. I have been using the above pre-match routine for years and have found it to be very effective.

Players experience different levels of tension when preparing for a match. If your tension level becomes elevated, take a series of deep breaths and remind yourself that tennis is only a game. You are here to enjoy the battle. Take the big load off your shoulders and find the joy in competing. Always remember, win or lose, it is all about the fun.

Twelve

It's Match Time: Be an
Intelligent Competitor

Your goal in a match is to develop and implement the most effective game plan that gives you the best opportunity to win. You have to play smart—it may become a chess match. You may make a move, and your opponent may make a countermove. Be prepared and remain focused and aggressive. You have to be an intelligent competitor. This chapter should help you understand some of the different strategies you can use to accomplish this.

To be an intelligent competitor, you need to do more than just evaluate your opponent's game—you need to have a clear understanding of your own game. Some areas of your game are likely stronger than others. For example, the best part of my game is my net game, but I am susceptible to footwork problems across the baseline. At six-foot-six, I have a larger body to move side to side when executing ground strokes. In the latter stages of a match, fatigue can set in. A few years ago I was playing a match against a player who had excellent ground strokes. He placed the tennis ball extremely well, and I was having a very difficult time breaking his serve. I ended up losing the first set, and I realized I needed to make a strategic change. Early in the match, he was placing his ground strokes so well that I was running from corner to corner, losing the majority of the rallies. I began to tire. I knew that I needed to shorten the points, so I decided to "chip and charge" (moving my weight through the return of serve and approaching the net as quickly as possible) on the return of serve. All of a sudden he became rattled and started to miss some passing shots, and I was finally able to break his serve. In this match I realized that if I stayed back at the baseline after my return, my chance of breaking his serve was almost nonexistent.

Let's take a look at another example. We will assume that your forehand is your best stroke. Every opportunity you have, you will need to consistently move around your backhand and position yourself to hit your forehand ground stroke. You want to hit as many forehands as possible. This will give you the opportunity to play your very best tennis.

As we discussed earlier, make sure you make a concerted effort to eliminate any glaring weaknesses in your game.

This should be your first plan of attack. A smart opponent will devise his game plan around any obvious deficiency. In the first few years I played, I possessed a very strong first serve but a very slow, ineffective second serve. I realized that to progress, I needed to develop a penetrating second serve with spin. It took time and practice, but my second serve significantly improved over the next six months. It was a great investment. If you have a weak backhand, volley, serve, or any other stroke, invest the time and energy to improve it. Removing an obvious weakness will have a positive impact on your game.

Your goal as a competitor is to take the offensive position in a match. This begins by identifying your opponent's strengths and weaknesses in the warm-up. A player may have a very strong two-handed backhand, for instance, but be prone to errors on his forehand side. In this case you need to try to make him hit as many forehands as possible. You should even make it obvious that you will be consistently hitting to his weaker side. Consequently he may experience a heightened level of anxiety, resulting in his forehand side becoming more vulnerable as the match progresses.

If you do end up losing the first set, you need to try to assess what went wrong and make a strategic change for the second. If you are playing doubles, you may want to lob more or use signals for poaching. You may both decide that you just need to be more consistent, keeping more balls in play. You want to implement a strategy that will hope-fully allow you to experience a shift in the momentum. Remember, even when you lose the first set in singles or doubles, there still is a lot of tennis to be played. Make a change or two and keep on fighting.

If you're the one who's winning, you need to stick with that winning game until your opponent can develop a plan to thwart it. Oftentimes a player will win the first set and then have a letdown in the beginning of the second. Before you know it, he is down 0–3 and needs to regroup to get back into the set. What happens at the beginning of the second set is that a player loses his sense of urgency. He ei-ther loses his focus and concentration or moves away from the game plan that was working for him in the first set. In tennis you have to keep your foot on the gas pedal from the first to the last point. If you played very aggressively in the first set and won, play the same way in the second. Never abandon a winning game.

I would like to expand on a key point mentioned in an earlier chapter. To play an intelligent tennis match, you need to have the mind-set that your strokes will consis-tently clear the net. It is very simple: if you hit the ball up and over the net, something positive can happen, but if you hit the ball in the net, nothing happens—the point is over. How many times in doubles do your opponents hit the ball in the air when your shot would be sailing long? Thus they keep you in the point. This happens more frequently than you may think. Try to make sure you clear the net consistently. Maintaining this thought process during the match does make a positive difference.

To become a better tennis player, you have to have a firm grasp on how to close out a set or match. A number of years ago I was ahead 5–4 in the third set in a tournament match, and it was my turn to serve. I remember telling myself that I really wanted to win this match and here was my opportunity. I didn't want the game score to get to 5–5, because my opponent had a great serve and an explosive forehand. Suddenly I began to rush between points and play very defensively. This resulted in a fairly quick loss of serve. After that I became very disappointed because I didn't play a smart game when I had the opportunity to close out the match. I went on to lose 7–5 in the third set.

What I needed to do was to focus on playing a strong game with the style of play that had put me in this favorable position in the first place. When you get to the point of closing out a set or match, eliminate any outcome-oriented thoughts. Make sure you concentrate on playing a strong game, utilizing the strategies and style of play that got you to this position. Then, if you do lose this game, it will be a lot easier to accept. Also, if it does end up 5–5, you need to stay positive and keep fighting. The match is far from over. Today when I am in the position to close out a match, I increase my positive self-talk, like *I play my best tennis at this point in a match* or *It is time for me to take my game to the next level.* These positive thoughts help me to stay relaxed and become more confident that I will play well. I may end up losing, but there is a strong chance it will not be due to my tennis, but rather to my opponent's play. I have been engaging in this type of self-talk for years when closing out a match, and I have seen the positive results it has had on my game.

To give yourself the best opportunity to succeed, you have to become an intelligent competitor. Employ any strategy that could potentially place you in a winning position. The next time you play, try to implement some of the strategies discussed in this chapter. This will help you to begin moving in the right direction. Review the section on closing out a match. It is so important to concentrate on playing aggressively, because it is very easy to become defensive in this stage of the match. Stay positive, and always implement your rituals.

Thirteen

DEVELOPING A MENTALLY
TOUGH DOUBLES TEAM

Doubles is such a great game to play. You have two players trying their best to work together toward a common goal. In this chapter, I want to develop a clear understanding of the qualities needed to become a mentally tough doubles team. Implementing these qualities will give your team the opportunity to consistently play your best game of doubles.

Both players should:

1) Be compatible
2) Be on time and prepared
3) Always stay positive
4) Participate in open and consistent communication

5) Share the same doubles strategy
6) Function as a team
7) Be flexible
8) Provide words of encouragement
9) Always give 100 percent effort
10) Win or lose as a team

1. Be compatible

First and foremost, to have any chance at consistent success, partners need to get along. You have to be comfortable with each other or you both may become unapproachable. You will simply stay on your side of the court and play without functioning as a team. Always remember, to be a great doubles team, you have to work together. This is much easier to accomplish if both players are compatible.

2. Be on time and prepared

When you become a team, there is an unspoken commitment that you will be at the match on time and prepared. At a minimum, you should arrive at your match forty-five minutes ahead of time. It is unfair to your partner to show up five or ten minutes late. This creates a stressful atmosphere and may result in poor play. Respect your partner because you are in this together.

Also, you need to be prepared for the match. Always make sure you have at least two rackets—you never know when you might break a string. Other items that may be necessary are tennis balls, water, a towel, wristbands, and extra clothing. It is a good idea to take a couple of bananas and an energy bar, and make sure you stay hydrated.

3. Always stay positive

To be a mentally tough doubles team, you have to stay positive even when faced with adversity. Both players need to stay focused on each and every point. If one player becomes discouraged, the team suffers. Remember what we talked about earlier: the scoring system always gives you an opportunity to come back in a match. One thing I do want to make clear here is that it is not your partner's responsibility to keep you positive and motivated—you have to take ownership of this for yourself. Both players need to stay upbeat and positive the entire match, and any communication between partners needs to be positive as well.

4. Participate in open and consistent communication

A strong doubles team engages in effective communication. Both players are very approachable and open to proposing any needed shift in strategy to each other. It is important that the lines of communication are wide open. At times teammates may have a difference of opinion on implementing a specific strategic change, but a strong doubles team quickly decides on a workable solution and gets right back to playing the match. Make sure you communicate frequently. This helps to ensure that you both are following the same game plan.

5. Share the same doubles strategy

In order for a team to be successful, each player has to share the same strategy of play. If one player wants the team to consistently approach the net and his partner wants to remain at the baseline, the chances of this team being successful are almost nonexistent. Both players need to possess the same vision of how doubles is played. If they don't, they may want to begin their search for new partners.

6. Function as a team

This is so important. Doubles is not two people playing singles, but rather two players working together to achieve a common goal. Their strength is dependent upon their ability to function as a team. Great teams move together, understand how to cover the middle ball, and how to handle the lob. They know where to be on the court in almost any situation. To be a good doubles team, you both need to have a firm grasp on how the game is played.

7. Be flexible

There are times where your partner will be struggling with some part of her game during a match. Subsequently she may ask you to make a strategic change that you are uncomfortable with. For example, suppose your partner is having a difficult time returning serve. She may ask you to move back to the baseline when it is her turn to return serve. This pushes you farther away from the net, resulting in some discomfort. Here is where you need to be flexible. You are a team, and as her partner you need to help her to alleviate her stress. Be flexible, and remember that it takes both of you playing well to give your team the best opportunity to win.

8. Provide words of encouragement

There are times when making a strategic change will not be enough to turn a match around. Maybe one player on the team is simply not playing well. This is when the partner has to stay upbeat and positive. A few words of encouragement to your partner would be advisable. It is unbelievable how a few uplifting words can go such a long way.

9. Always give 100 percent effort

To give your team the best opportunity to be successful, you have to give 100 percent effort at all times. Remember, if you don't give a maximum level of effort, you are letting down your partner and yourself. You are a team. You cannot control winning and losing, but you can control the level of effort you give on each point. You owe it to yourself and your partner to keep fighting.

10. Win or lose as a team

It is very important that you don't blame a loss on your partner. You are a team. Maybe your partner didn't play well, but you made mistakes too. Both players need to take ownership for the loss and refrain from pointing the finger at each other. When you blame your partner, it is simply a sign of insecurity in yourself. It may also end up breaking up a good doubles team, and worse, a friendship.

If you are going to play with a particular partner for a period of time, make sure the above concepts are in order. It will get your team started in the right direction. Committing to these keys gives you the best opportunity to be successful as a team. You won't end up just being two individuals attempting to play the game of doubles together. You will function as a team, and this will give you the best chance at consistent success.

Fourteen

Selecting a Teaching Professional

It is very important that you select the right professional to join you on your tennis journey. Who you employ can have a major impact on your future progress. Like any other occupation, there is a wide range of ability among certified teaching professionals. It is important to take a lesson from a few different professionals before you make your final decision.

Below are the important characteristics you need to look for before you make your selection. Your tennis professional should be:

Approachable	A good listener
Positive	A good teacher
Friendly	Passionate about the game

| Understanding | Full of energy |
| Knowledgeable | Interested in your improvement |

These are the main attributes to consider prior to making your final decision. It is very important that you feel comfortable discussing your tennis goals with the person you select. Whether you are experiencing excessive pressure when you compete or are unable to execute a low volley, you need to share common goals for your game. Frequent communication is critical because attaining these goals is a joint venture. You both should have a clear understanding of where you are now and where you would like to be in the near future.

For you to improve on a consistent basis, your teaching professional has to be very knowledgeable about the game and possess excellent teaching skills. During the selection process, note well how each candidate meets these two criteria.

Remember, if the teaching candidate is passionate about the game, there is a good chance he or she will become passionate about *your* game. The instructor will take ownership for each lesson you have together. He or she will take pride in your accomplishments and become an integral part of your tennis experience.

Let's assume that you have found the perfect candidate and are moving forward with lessons. As the student, you have a major responsibility. Once a lesson has been completed, you have to find time during the week to practice what you worked on. Remember, in order to progress, you need to develop the skills you practiced in the lesson. Your teaching professional is an excellent instructor, but he's not a magician. He cannot wave a magic wand and suddenly give you a serve like Serena Williams's. You have to practice.

Finally, your choice for a teaching professional will have a major impact on your future progress. Take the time to interview some candidates, and consider the above attributes as a blueprint for the type of instructor you are looking for. Best of luck!

Fifteen

The Fortunate Ones

Are you concerned about losing your spot on your USTA team, or are you developing a fear of losing? Are you worrying about your rating or ranking, or are you afraid to let your partner down? The list of worries can go on and on. Let me tell you, sometimes you have to take a step back and remember what the game is all about. You have to be happy that you are simply able to play. Your knees, ankles, elbows, and other body parts are holding up, so you are able to participate in the great game of tennis. It might not always be so.

Earlier in this book I mentioned my mentor, Jim Oyer, who became a dear friend of mine and has remained so for many years. His passion for the game of tennis is unsurpassed. He loved to play and looked forward to every opportunity he had to get out on the court. I came to the point where I shared his passion. Today Jim is in his mid-seventies and finds it very difficult to play anymore. We try to meet every year to catch up on what is going on in our lives. When we meet, Jim reflects on the different matches and tournaments we won. It is amazing how he remembers whom we played and in what city. We only meet for a few days, and the time seems to pass quickly. Last time, as he was walking out the door to return home, I got a tear in my eye. I began to think about how tennis was such an important part of his life, and now all he has is the memories. It made me realize that there will be a day when I will have to put my racket in my tennis bag for the last time. It was a sad feeling because I, like Jim, have developed a true love for the game. I reminded myself to continue to have fun and be thankful for each and every time I am able to walk out on the court.

Earlier I mentioned the foot operation that sidelined me for a few weeks. Two physicians informed me that the likelihood of my being able to play tennis again at my current level after I recover from the operation is remote. Sure, this is disheartening, but I take solace in the fact that I will still be able to play. I will be able to continue to enjoy the game that has become an integral part of my life over the past forty years. Some people only have great memories of the pleasure they had when playing this great game. We who can still play are truly the fortunate ones.

You need to enjoy the experience when you play, because there will come a day when you will have to set your racket aside. When reflecting back on your tennis life, are you going to be able to recall many of the wonderful times you experienced on the tennis court, or are you going to remember the unnecessary worry and pressure you placed on yourself? It is all up to you. You and you alone are in control of your tennis destiny. If self-imposed worries and pressures have controlled your life, you can make a change today. You can begin the first day of your new tennis life and find pleasure in competing again. It is up to you.

Sixteen

My Final Thoughts

First, I'd like to thank you for reading my book. I am very thankful that I was introduced to the great game of tennis over forty years ago. I have always been passionate about the game, and I have truly enjoyed teaching and playing competitively. Even though I have faced a number of mental struggles, I wouldn't trade my tennis experience for anything.

In this book I have discussed the ways I have dealt with the stress and pressures of competition. Improving your mental game takes time, but with some perseverance you can take this part of your game to the next level. Make sure you enjoy your tennis experiences. Roger Federer recently said, "Sometimes you're just happy playing. Some people, some media, unfortunately don't understand that it's okay just to play tennis and enjoy it. They always think you have to win everything, [that] it always needs to be a success story, and if it's not, obviously, what is the point? Maybe you have to go back and think, why have I started playing tennis? Because I just like it…It's actually sort of a dream hobby that became somewhat of a job. Some people just don't get that, ever."

Don't get caught up in ratings, rankings, or reputation. *You* are the central focus of your competitive game. You and only you are the master of your tennis destiny. Place all your tennis worries in a box and throw away the key. Don't be held hostage by them for one more day. Remove the tension indicators so you can relax and play your best tennis. Taking some deep breaths between points and on changeovers will greatly assist in this.

Don't base your confidence solely on the roller coaster ride of winning and losing. Make the effort to base your confidence on controllable behaviors. This will allow you to enjoy the game so much more. Put into practice the five simple concentration keys. They are very effective and easy to implement. Focus on improving both the mental and physical aspects of your game by setting some performance-based goals, which you can control, rather than outcome-based goals, which you cannot control.

Choose the right teaching professional by being patient with the selection process. It is extremely important to find the right person to develop your game with you. This has such a major impact on how quickly you will improve.

Be thankful that you are physically able to play this great game. There are so many people who are not fortunate enough to be able to play tennis. Finally, the day will come when you will put your racket in your tennis bag for the last time. On this day, I hope you will be able to say, "Tennis was one of the best experiences of my life." This is what the game is really all about!

About the Author

S teve Brady received a BA in psychology and an MS in counselor education from Alfred University in Alfred, New York. He is a certified elite professional with the US Professional Tennis Association and a certified professional with the Professional Tennis Registry. Steve served as the head tennis professional at Palmetto Dunes Tennis Center of Hilton Head Island and the Wild Dunes Tennis Center of the Isle of Palms, both in South Carolina. At these facilities, he supervised up to fifteen teaching professionals during their main season.

Steve's recent tennis accomplishments include being ranked number one in the Adult 50 & Over division in 2008 and 2010 by the Southern Section of the United States Tennis Association. In 2013 he was ranked number one in the Adult 55 & Over division by the Florida Section of the USTA. He received the United States Tennis Professional Association's 2014 Player of the Year award for the 50 & Over division, and he served as captain of the West Coast 55s Florida Cup team for the 2014 and 2015 competitions.

Steve and his wife, Mary, currently reside in Tampa, where he manages a tennis-teaching business. He has two children, Chris and Steve, and a daughter-in-law, Rosy. Besides tennis, Steve enjoys basketball and fitness training. Steve can be reached via his website at www.stevebradytennis.com and emails can be sent to stevenbrady06@gmail.com.

Notes

Notes

Made in the USA
Middletown, DE
21 January 2021